EFFECTIVE
PERFORMANCE
APPRAISALS

EFFECTIVE
PERFORMANCE
APPRAISALS

Robert B Maddux

KOGAN
PAGE

Copyright © Crisp Publications Inc 1987

First published in the United States of America
in 1986, revised 1987, by Crisp Publications Inc, 95 First Street,
Los Altos, California 94022, USA

This edition first published in Great Britain in
1988 by Kogan Page Ltd, 120 Pentonville Road,
London N1 9JN

British Library Cataloguing in Publication Data

Maddux, Robert B.
    Effective performance appraisals.
    1. Employees, Rating of
    I. Title
    658.3′125   HF5549.5.R3

    ISBN 1-85091-552-0
    ISBN 1-85091-553-9 Pbk

Typeset by DP Photosetting, Aylesbury, Bucks
Printed and bound in Great Britain by
Dotesios (Printers) Ltd, Bradford-on-Avon, Wiltshire

Contents

Contents

Preface

This book is for anyone who directs the activities of others. Whether a first line supervisor, the chairperson of a committee, a project leader, a school administrator, a restaurant manager, a government official, the owner of a small business, or a senior executive, you must be able to discuss performance effectively with those who report to you.

Leading a performance appraisal review can be either difficult and depressing, or dynamic and positive. The attitude, planning, and approach of the person conducting the review will make the difference.

This book will help you to think through the appraisal process, and then learn how to conduct discussions that encourage positive relationships and improved individual performances. Those who master the concepts presented will benefit from reduced stress and improved productivity.

You will have a chance to do some self-analysis which will identify personal strengths and weaknesses. Once learned, the application of the skills is up to you.

Robert B Maddux

PART 1

Are You Ready for Better Appraisals?

CHAPTER 1
Some Objectives for the Reader

Before you begin this book, give some thought to your objectives.

Objectives give us a sense of direction, a definition of what we plan to accomplish, and a feeling of fulfilment when they are achieved.

Check the objectives that are important to you. Then, when you have completed the book, review your objectives and enjoy the sense of achievement you will feel.

After reading and practising the concepts in this book, you will be able to:

- establish a work climate conducive to productive performance appraisals;
- initiate and maintain positive communication about work performance versus work expectations;
- help your employees prepare properly for performance appraisal;
- prepare and conduct performance discussions that encourage an exchange of information and produce better results;
- follow through properly on agreements reached with the employee.

> *A performance appraisal provides an opportunity for communication between the person who assigns the work and the person who performs it, to discuss what they expect from the other and how well those expectations are being met.*
>
> Performance appraisals are not adversarial proceedings, or social chit-chat. They are an essential communication link between two people with a common purpose.
>
> Leading these discussions is not always easy, but the principles and techniques for effective sessions can be learned and applied by anyone.

MEET SOME SUCCESSES AND SOME FAILURES

CHAPTER 2
Make Your Choice Now

Successes

Leaders who engage in mutual goal setting.

Leaders who publicly recognise positive performance, and privately correct improper performance when it occurs.

Leaders who establish clear, measurable expectations, and provide a climate conducive to success.

Leaders who ask questions, listen carefully and appreciate the ideas of others.

Leaders who follow through to ensure commitments are met.

Add from your own experience:

_____

_____

_____

_____

Failures

Those who establish arbitrary, unilateral performance goals and/or standards.

Those who spend too much time looking for things that are wrong and too little looking for things that are right.

Those who have not thought through what they expect or don't know how to measure success. Those who provide a threatening atmosphere in which to work.

Those who never seek the ideas of others or listen, yet have a solution for everyone else's problems.

Those who do not take their own commitments seriously.

Add from your own experience:

_____

_____

_____

_____

A good performance appraisal leaves both parties feeling they have gained something.

Do you tend to put off performance appraisals?

Too often performance appraisals are left until the last minute and then done in a hurried manner. When this occurs, the results are poor. The supervisor feels guilty, and the employee unimportant and let down.

The page opposite lists several advantages of conducting thoughtful performance appraisals when they are due. Tick those that are important to you.

ADVANTAGES OF DOING A GOOD JOB

CHAPTER 3

What Can Well Planned Performance Appraisals Do for Me?

People responsible for performance appraisals often assign a low priority to them because they have not thought about the benefits of a good appraisal session. Some advantages of doing a professional appraisal on a regular basis are given below. Tick ☑ those that are important to you.

☐ 1. Performance appraisals give me valuable insights into the work being done and those who are doing it.

☐ 2. When I maintain good communication with others about job expectations and results, opportunities are created for new ideas and improved methods.

☐ 3. When I do a good job appraising performance, anxiety is reduced because employees know how they are doing.

☐ 4. I increase productivity when employees receive regular corrective feedback on their performance.

☐ 5. I reinforce sound work practices and encourage good performance when I publicly recognise positive contributions.

☐ 6. When I encourage two way communication with employees, goals are clarified so they can be achieved or exceeded.

☐ 7. Regular appraisal sessions remove surprises about how the quality of work is being perceived.

☐ 8. Learning to conduct professional performance appraisals is excellent preparation for advancement and increased responsibility.

Research shows that more than half the professional and clerical employees working today do not understand how their work is evaluated. If this could be true of your employees, familiarise them with the process now and tell all new employees how they will be evaluated when they begin work.

Performance appraisal discussions are normally initiated by the supervisor, but are also appropriate when employees request a meeting to find out how well you think they are doing.

OPPORTUNITIES FOR APPRAISAL DISCUSSION

CHAPTER 4

Opportunities for Performance Appraisals

Tick ☑ those that apply to you.

☐ 1. Appraisal discussions should be scheduled on a regular basis either as organisational policy or by the supervisor.

☐ 2. Less formal discussions may be conducted whenever the nature of the assignment or other circumstances make it meaningful to do so.

☐ 3. Leaders should provide praise for achievement whenever appropriate and take prompt action to correct unsatisfactory performance when it occurs.

☐ 4. Appraisal activities handled at a propitious moment may be recalled later during a more formal, scheduled review for reinforcement.

☐ 5. Follow-up discussions after a formal appraisal provide the opportunity for a broader review if needed.

Case Study 1
Who will be the best at performance appraisals?

Case studies provide insights about the content that has been, or is about to be, presented.

The first case (below) will help you understand some of the ground work necessary to achieve a successful performance appraisal.

Janice and Frank are new supervisors attending their first training workshop. They have not yet covered material on performance appraisals, but are discussing their personal philosophies about them over lunch. Janice doesn't believe a fair performance appraisal can be made of an employee's work unless assignments have been discussed, and expectations agreed upon in advance. She thinks work should be assigned in measurable terms so both she and the employee can track performance as the work progresses.

Frank thinks this approach is dangerous. He feels employees should be given only a general idea of what is to be accomplished. He thinks employees who participate in establishing performance objectives will set them too low. He prefers to leave performance expectations vague to see what the employees accomplish on their own. If their standards don't measure up, he will let them know then and there.

Who do you think will be the best at performance appraisals?

☐ Janice
Because _____

_____

☐ Frank
Because _____

_____

Turn to page 73 for the author's views.

PART 2

How to Prepare for
More Effective Appraisals

CHAPTER 5

What is Meant by Goals and Standards?

The appraisal process starts when the employee and supervisor reach a mutual understanding of what needs to be accomplished. If expectations are not clearly stated, mutually understood and presented in measurable terms, performance will be difficult to evaluate.

Goals and standards are methods by which job expectations can be expressed. Those responsible for performance appraisals need a good understanding of goals and standards, and how to use them during the appraisal process.

If you agree with the definitions and examples below, tick ☑ the appropriate boxes.

Goals

☐ A goal is a statement of results which are to be achieved. Goals describe: (1) conditions that will exist when the desired outcome has been accomplished; (2) a time frame during which the outcome is to be completed; and (3) resources the organisation is willing to commit to achieve the desired result.

Goals should be challenging, but achievable and established with the participation of those responsible for meeting them. Here is an example:

'To increase the flow of invoices through the Accounts Department to a minimum of 150 per day by 1 October. The total increased cost to accomplish this should not exceed £550.'

Once accomplished, a new goal can be established to emphasise the next set of desired results.

Standards

□   A standard refers to an ongoing performance criterion that must be met time and time again. Standards are usually expressed quantitatively, and refer to such things as attendance, breakage, manufacturing tolerances, production rates and safety standards. They are most effective when established with the participation of those who must meet them. Here is an example:

> *'The departmental filing backlog should not exceed one week. Any record requested should be available within five minutes of the request.'*

In general, goals apply more to managers and professional employees who engage in individualised projects. Standards are more common for workers engaged in routine, repetitive tasks.

When employees participate in setting goals and standards, there should be no mystery about how their performance will be judged. Employees cannot say, 'Why didn't you tell me that's what you wanted?' or, 'Who dreamed up these impossible standards?'

Since goals and/or standards are the primary criteria by which performance will be measured, it is worth reviewing them. Complete the exercise below.

Identifying goals and standards

In the following list of statements, place a G if it is a goal and an S in the box if it is a standard according to the definitions on pages 21 and 22. If the statement is neither a goal nor a standard, leave the □ blank. Answers are at the bottom of the page.

☐ 1. Breakage in the kitchen should be kept to a minimum.

☐ 2. To eliminate maintenance coding errors for existing computer programs by 1 October, at a cost not to exceed 40 working hours.

☐ 3. Reduce the cost of ongoing operations by 1 January.

☐ 4. Telephones are to be answered quickly and messages taken when necessary.

☐ 5. To reduce burner maintenance cost by 15 per cent before 15 November, at a once and for all cost not to exceed £10,000.

☐ 6. To increase sales of men's watches by 10 per cent before 1 June, with no increase in costs.

☐ 7. Appreciably reduce time lost because of accidents by year end.

☐ 8. Errors in recording class enrolment will not exceed 2% of the total monthly enrolment.

☐ 9. Telephones should be answered after no more than two rings. Telephone manners are expected to follow those prescribed in the company handbook. Messages should include date, time of call, relevant names and numbers, and the nature of the call.

☐ 10. To increase Western Region sales by £200,000, by year end, at an increased cost of sales of less than 5 per cent.

Answers

Items 2, 5, 6 and 10 are measurable goals.
Items 8 and 9 are measurable standards.
Items 1, 3, 4 and 7 are neither goals nor standards.

Our attitude towards people determines our approach to performance appraisals

Some leaders conduct performance appraisals well because their attitude towards people sets them on a positive course. Others are less successful because their attitude creates a negative climate. The next page describes three different attitudes. Which one best describes you?

CHAPTER 6
Attitudes and Performance Appraisals

Tick ☑ the one that best describes you

☐ *'I know best.'* This person feels work should be done by controlling the people who do it. Workers are told what to do, how to do it, and when to stop. Then they are told what they did wrong and what they did right; where they are weak, and where they are strong. The person in charge feels this is justified because of his or her superior knowledge and ability. This attitude does not invite new ideas or challenge people. Communication is directed one way only.

☐ *'I'll set the goals, you meet them.'* This person feels that because of superior knowledge, ability or experience, it is OK to set goals for others to meet. The worker is given an opportunity to discuss ways to meet goals, but has no input into the actual performance objectives. Performance is evaluated on how well original goals were achieved, regardless of how realistic they were.

☐ *'Let's review the work together, establish some realistic goals and evaluate performance accordingly.'* This person emphasises work performance, not worker characteristics. The idea is to help workers evaluate the usefulness of their ideas; recognise their weaknesses; and exploit their strengths. The leader acts as a resource and enabler, rather than as a judge.

SELF-ANALYSIS

Personal characteristics influence how we perform as appraisers. Now is a good time to evaluate your appraisal skills. Complete the assessment opposite.

Commit yourself now to improving your skills in any area indicated by your ratings.

CHAPTER 7
Characteristics of an Effective Appraiser

The following personal characteristics support effective performance appraisals. This scale will help identify your strengths, and indicate areas where improvement would be beneficial. Circle the number that best reflects where you fall on the scale. The higher the number, the more the characteristic describes you. When you have finished, total the numbers circled in the space provided.

1.	I like being responsible for productivity.	10 9 8 7 6 5 4 3 2 1
2.	I like people, and enjoy talking to them.	10 9 8 7 6 5 4 3 2 1
3.	I don't mind giving criticism of a constructive nature.	10 9 8 7 6 5 4 3 2 1
4.	I give praise freely when it is earned.	10 9 8 7 6 5 4 3 2 1
5.	I am not intimidated by workers who tell me what they really think.	10 9 8 7 6 5 4 3 2 1
6.	I seek new ideas and use them whenever possible.	10 9 8 7 6 5 4 3 2 1
7.	I respect the knowledge and skill of the people who work for me.	10 9 8 7 6 5 4 3 2 1
8.	I follow up to be sure commitments, goals and standards are being met.	10 9 8 7 6 5 4 3 2 1
9.	I am sensitive to the needs and feelings of others.	10 9 8 7 6 5 4 3 2 1
10.	I am not worried by employees who know more about their work than I do.	10 9 8 7 6 5 4 3 2 1

TOTAL _____

A score between 90 and 100 indicates you have excellent characteristics to conduct effective appraisals. A score between 70 and 89 indicates that you have significant strengths, but also some improvement needs, Scores between 50 and 69 reflect a significant number of problem areas. Scores below 50 call for a serious effort to improve. Make a special effort to grow in any area where you scored 6 or less, regardless of your total score.

Preparation by an employee for the appraisal discussion is as important as preparation by the manager.

The appraisal discussion should be a structured and planned interpersonal meeting, not a casual conversation.

A specific time, agreeable to both parties, should be reserved.

Topics for discussion should be known in advance so the participants can prepare accordingly.

Help employees to prepare by providing them with an advance copy of 'Thought Stimulators For Self-Appraisal' printed on the next page.

CHAPTER 8

Thought Stimulators for Self-appraisal

These questions can help you prepare for your performance appraisal. As you read each question, think about your performance, your progress, and your plans for future growth.

1. What critical abilities does my job require? To what extent do I fulfil them?
2. What do I like best about my job? Least?
3. What were my specific accomplishments during this appraisal period?
4. Which goals or standards did I fall short of meeting?
5. How could my supervisor help me do a better job?
6. Is there anything that the organisation or my supervisor does that hinders my effectiveness?
7. What changes would improve my performance?
8. Does my present job make the best use of my capabilities? How could I become more productive?
9. Do I need more experience or training in any aspect of my current job? How could it be accomplished?
10. What have I done since my last appraisal to prepare myself for more responsibility?
11. What new goals and standards should be established for the next appraisal period? Which old ones need to be modified or deleted?
12. What do I expect to be doing five years from now?

A tip on how to get started:

THOROUGH PREPARATION BY THE MANAGER!

> When a performance appraisal goes poorly, it is usually
> because the supervisor has not prepared properly, or
> completely, or has not given the employee the opportunity
> to prepare.

BE PREPARED ➡

CHAPTER 9

Managerial Preparation for Planning the Appraisal

Prior to conducting a performance appraisal, identify and develop items to be covered. Since employee performance in the current job is the central issue, gather relevant information concerning job requirements and the established goals or standards. Next, assess the employee's performance on the above for the appraisal period. Then:

1. Review the job requirements to be sure you are fully conversant with them.
2. Review the goals and standards you previously discussed and agreed upon with the employee (plus any notes you have relating to their achievement).
3. Review the employee's history including:
   — job skills
   — training
   — experience
   — special or unique qualifications
   — past jobs and job performance.
4. Evaluate job performance versus job expectations for the period being appraised, and rate it from unacceptable to outstanding.
5. Note any variances in the employee's performance that need to be discussed. Provide specific examples.
6. Consider career opportunities or limitations for this person. Be prepared to discuss them.

CHAPTER 10
Pitfalls to Avoid

Factors that mislead or blind us when we are in the appraisal process are pitfalls to be avoided. An appraiser must be on guard against anything that distorts reality favourably or unfavourably. Some typical pitfalls include:

- Bias/Prejudice. Things we tend to react to that have nothing to do with performance such as: race, religion, education, family background, age and/or sex.
- Trait assessment. Too much attention to characteristics that have nothing to do with the job and are difficult to measure. Examples include characteristics such as flexibility, sincerity, or friendliness.
- Over-emphasis on favourable or unfavourable performance of one or two tasks which could lead to an unbalanced evaluation of the overall contribution.
- Relying on impressions rather than facts.
- Holding the employee responsible for the effect of factors beyond his or her control.
- Failure to provide each employee with an opportunity for advance preparation.

> Concentrate on performance measured against mutually understood expectations.

In an appraisal discussion, four fundamental areas need to be covered:

1. The measurement of results of the employee's performance against goals and/or standards.
2. Recognition of the employee's contributions.
3. Correction of any new or ongoing performance problems.
4. The establishment of goals and/or standards for the next appraisal period.

Everything of substance during the discussion should relate to these elements, and both parties should actively participate in the discussion. A plan, prepared in advance, will help keep the discussion on target.

Develop an action plan for the discussion.

HERE'S HOW ➡

CHAPTER 11
How to Develop an Action Plan

Once you have completed your planning review, you will need to develop an action plan for the appraisal. Keep the following guidelines in mind and tick ☑ those you expect to use in your action plan.

☐ 1. Don't cover too many areas in any one discussion. Concentrate on those which deserve the most attention.

☐ 2. Make sure there are specific, unbiased examples that can be used to support your points but that also allow for dialogue.

☐ 3. Develop positive approaches to correcting problems. Give the employee an opportunity to suggest solutions before any final decisions are made.

☐ 4. Be prepared to provide praise and positive reinforcement for items which deserve it.

☐ 5. Identify developmental activities that will improve the employee's performance in the present assignment; and/or provide preparation for future assignments.

☐ 6. Note any projects, goals and/or standards to be accomplished during the forthcoming appraisal period. Discuss them and reach agreement on them during the session.

☐ 7. Plan to involve the employee in all aspects of the discussion.

OUTSTANDING? SATISFACTORY? UNSATISFACTORY?

Your conclusions from the evaluation should be a primary guide to structure the appraisal discussion. Read on for some suggested approaches.

HAVE YOUR DISCUSSION OBJECTIVES WELL IN MIND AS YOU PREPARE.

APPRAISAL MODELS

CHAPTER 12
Appraisal Discussion Models

Your overall evaluation of an employee will range from outstanding to unsatisfactory. Select an approach to your appraisal discussion that is in keeping with your evaluation. The employee, for example, may be outstanding in the current assignment, but not promotable because certain key skills are lacking. You have to decide how to handle each case. Some possible discussion models are given below.

End Result of Evaluation	Employee's Likely Future	Discussion Objective
Outstanding	Promotion	Consider opportunities
	Growth in present assignment	Make development plans
	Broadened assignment	Review possibility of extending responsibility
	No change in duties	How to maintain performance level
Satisfactory	Promotion	Consider possibilities
	Growth in present assignment	Make development plans
	No change in duties	How to maintain or improve performance level
Unsatisfactory	Performance correctible	Plan correction and gain commitment
	Performance uncorrectible	Review possible re-assignment, or prepare for termination

Case Study 2:
What upset Jack?

Now is a good time to apply what you have read. Analyse the case study below based on what you have learned.

Diana has just completed a performance appraisal discussion with one of her employees and is upset about it. She told another supervisor at lunch, 'I appraised Jack this morning. I had to call him out of the budget meeting because I remembered all my appraisals were due today. I couldn't believe his reaction. He said he had no time to prepare, and expected me to have an example to support each criticism I made. About all he did, really, was to criticise my position on a couple of issues. I told him several things I didn't like about his performance, and then was good enough to tell him how to correct his faults. All I got back was anger and silence. You would think he would be grateful for some feedback, but I guess people today don't really care about improving. Normally he's a pretty good employee, but he was very upset during the appraisal. What do you suppose is wrong with him?'

Please use the space below to write down what you think is 'wrong' with Jack. Check your answer with the author's on page 73.

_____

_____

_____

_____

_____

_____

_____

_____

_____

PART 3

Conducting the Appraisal

CHAPTER 13
How to Begin the Appraisal Discussion

Managers have the responsibility to initiate appraisal discussions. Although individual personalities will influence the format, experts agree that the discussion should be held in a private place to avoid interruptions and should begin on a positive and friendly note. While chit-chat will help break the ice, both parties will welcome getting down to business.

One way to accomplish this is to highlight a specific positive achievement and discuss it first. Another approach is to ask the employee to review his or her accomplishments for the appraisal period. This allows the employee to select where to begin and can lead to a candid assessment of actual performance. While the employee is talking, the leader should be an interested listener.

If variances between expectations and results are evident, it is important that both leader and employee try to find out what they are and why they occurred. This helps the discussion become a joint problem solving session which can lead to the implementation of effective solutions.

The employee should be encouraged to identify as many reasons for variances as possible. None should be rejected out of hand even if they seem to be excuses. The leader should also contribute possible causes so that nothing significant is overlooked. This sharing allows for an exchange of viewpoints. This can provide better insights for all concerned and lead to a new understanding of the expectations of the organisation, and the people who staff it.

The leader must be sure that unsatisfactory performance is identified and discussed.

Experts believe that at least 50 per cent of performance problems in business occur because of lack of feedback. An employee will see no reason to change performance if it appears acceptable to the supervisor and the organisation.

Some ways to create constructive feedback, and maintain a climate conducive to a good outcome are given in the following pages.

NEVER IGNORE
UNSATISFACTORY
PERFORMANCE!

CHAPTER 14
Discussing Unsatisfactory Performance

Employees who work in a non-threatening atmosphere are more likely to discuss their shortcomings in the appraisal setting. When this occurs, the supervisor can be supportive by saying something like, 'That's very perceptive. What can we do to correct this situation?'

If the employee has been unsatisfactory in an aspect of his or her job, and does not bring up areas of weak performance, the supervisor must do so. It helps to be able to describe the impact of the poor performance on the organisation.

Some employees may not realise they are falling short of expectations. Or they may assume everything is acceptable because no one has ever discussed the problem with them. Sometimes they may feel everything is OK because they see others doing the same thing.

A first step to correct unsatisfactory performance is to review expectations. If the employee is unaware of these expectations, they must be made clear, and a commitment made that they will be met. If expectations are not being met for some other reason, the supervisor must first learn why, and then agree on a corrective action plan worked out with the employee.

Questions like these can be helpful in opening up the issues:

'Are you aware of the standards for quantity and quality we expect on this item?'

'Are you aware of your error rate versus the departmental average?'

'We seem to be running about two weeks behind schedule; can you tell me why, and what we can do to catch up?'

'Your sales reports are excellent but they are never on time. Can you explain why?'

'Fifty per cent of your staff resigned in the last quarter. To what do you attribute that?'

CHAPTER 15

How to Get an Employee to Talk Freely

> *Successful discussion leaders believe that employees should do most of the talking. This can be achieved by using good communication skills, and an atmosphere that encourages discussion.*

Employees often say very little during an appraisal discussion. There are several possible reasons for this, some include:

- The employee does not understand the purpose of the appraisal, and is afraid to express an opinion.
- The employee is not given the opportunity to express an opinion.
- The employee was not given time to prepare for the discussion.
- The employee's thoughts and ideas are quickly brushed aside or discounted.
- The employee feels the whole process is meaningless.

A manager can overcome this reluctance to enter into a dialogue by creating the right type of non-threatening atmosphere. Tick ☑ those methods you expect to use.

☐ 1. Be descriptive rather than judgemental

When a supervisor is judgemental about an employee's performance, it almost always brings out defensive behaviour. A better climate is established when descriptive terms are used to describe problems. This makes it possible for the leader and employee to discuss a solution unemotionally, or even better, a solution generated by the employee. Note the differences in the following example:

Judgemental	Descriptive
'How could you do such a silly thing?'	'Can you explain what caused the incident?'

Leaders who use descriptive, non-judgemental language in the appraisal discussion show a desire to analyse and resolve a problem, not to find a scapegoat or a way to demean the employee.

☐ 2. Be supportive, not authoritarian

Supervisors sometimes purposely, and sometimes inadvertently, display an authoritarian attitude during the discussion. This can create resentment and defensiveness. It is usually better to respect the employee's ability to contribute to the solution of a problem. Here is an example:

Authoritarian	Supportive
'Here is what we will do to get this done on time.'	'What do you suggest we do to get this done on time in the future?'

Supportive practices generate options for problem-solving because the employee is encouraged to make suggestions. They also focus on the problem, not the employee. In addition, a supportive approach promotes better listening by both parties, and permits a climate where disagreement is not only acceptable, but invited.

☐ 3. Reflect equality, not superiority

Supervisors who put too much emphasis on their position and power often create barriers between themselves and their employees. Supervisors who share information with employees and then seek their opinions provide a flavour of equality. Here is an example:

Superiority	Equality
'I was doing it this way before you were born.'	'We have done it this way for years but I would like to hear your ideas on how we can do it better.'

Employees appreciate a leader who shares information, asks for opinions and listens to ideas. Leaders who understand this have appraisal discussions that are more enlightening and productive.

☐ 4. Be accepting, not dogmatic

Supervisors who approach decisions, plans and problems dogmatically are telling employees there is no need for other ideas or solutions. Things have already been decided. This can demoralise an employee who has ideas and wants to excel. Leaders who listen to employee input, or allow their ideas to be challenged in a search for the best solution, stimulate enthusiasm, creativity and productivity. Here is an example that contrasts the two approaches:

Dogmatic	Accepting
'This is the best solution.'	'This is the best solution I could come up with. What other possibilities do you see?'

A supervisor who accepts employees' input recognises their value, capitalises on their knowledge and builds confidence in the group.

> SUPERVISORS LEARN MORE
> FROM LISTENING THAN
> TALKING!

Thoughtful questions can provide some very important side benefits, because:

- They require the leader's commitment to listen.
- They stimulate thought about specific issues.
- They solicit another person's ideas, point of view or feelings.
- They provide an opportunity to test an idea against the reasoning of someone else.
- They elicit important information that might not otherwise be available.

3 TYPES OF QUESTION ➡

CHAPTER 16

Questions that Facilitate Appraisal Discussions

There are three types of question that can be used to help the supervisor and employee better understand each other's point of view. Tick ☑ those you would feel comfortable using.

☐ 1. **Open questions.** Questions which cannot be answered with a yes or no. These questions require an opinion or expression of feeling. For example: 'What is your opinion of . . . ?'

> Advantages of open questions include:
>
> - a demonstration of your interest in the other person's point of view;
> - a confirmation that you value the other person's ideas and feelings;
> - a stimulation of thought about specific issues;
> - a better understanding of the other person's needs;
> - the encouragement of a dialogue rather than a monologue.

☐ 1. **Reflective questions.** A reflective question repeats a statement that the other person has made in the form of a question. Good listening skills are required. It is also important to select the most significant feeling or idea stated. For example:

Employee: 'Our results would be better if we modified the procedures used to take samples.'

Supervisor: 'You're convinced the results can be improved?'

Reflective questions can be helpful because:

- arguments can be avoided. You respond without accepting or rejecting what has been said.
- it confirms you understand what has been said. If you reflect incorrectly, the other party has an opportunity to correct you.
- the other person is encouraged to clarify or expand upon what has been said.
- the other person can recognise illogical statements they may have made if the statement comes back in a non-directive fashion.
- they create a dialogue conducive to agreement.

---

1. **Directive questions.** These are used to solicit information about a particular point or issue. Directive questions are usually reserved until after the other person has finished talking on the subject. Directive questions can then be used to sustain communication, or obtain information or ideas in which you are specifically interested. Here is an example:

Supervisor: 'If you are convinced the results can be improved, what steps would you take and when would you take them?'

Directive questions have these advantages:

- They provide pertinent information in those areas of greatest importance to you.
- They challenge the other person to explore ideas, defend statements, and contribute suggestions.
- They offer both parties specific facts on an issue.

Open, reflective and directive questions are all useful techniques to draw the employee into a thorough discussion of job performance and personal development.

The appraisal discussion is more than a simple review of job performance. It should progress naturally to a discussion of how the employee can do a better job in the future.

It is also a good time to draw out the employee's ambitions and aspirations.

CHAPTER 17
Personal Development and Growth

As performance is discussed, it often becomes apparent that additional training and development are required or desirable. It is also possible that the discussion will provide an indication that an employee is ready for more responsibility which requires new or improved skills.

Therefore, specific areas for improvement, and the need for new skill development should be discussed. Techniques by which further growth can be accomplished should also be covered. The leader should encourage the employee to talk about personal growth needs, so goals to meet them can be established. This effort can be supported by:

- Serving as a sounding board to explore developmental alternatives.
- Testing the extent to which the employee has thought through developmental objectives.
- Providing a supportive climate for learning.

The final employee development plans should be specific and include agreement by the employee for:

- What the employee needs to do.
- When the employee needs to do it.
- What the leader needs to do and when.
- Once development is completed, how it is to be applied.

CHARACTERISTICS OF AN EFFECTIVE
DISCUSSION LEADER

The appraiser's attitude towards the appraisal discussion
will make a genuine difference in the outcome. A well led
session provides an opportunity to share ideas, points of
view, and discuss problems and successes. Examine your
attitude on the next page.

SELF-ANALYSIS ➡️

CHAPTER 18
Characteristics of an Effective Discussion Leader

The characteristics on page 56 are essential to effective performance appraisal discussions. This scale will help you to identify strengths and determine areas where improvement would be beneficial. Circle the number that best reflects where you fall on the scale. The higher the number, the more you are like the characteristic. When you have finished, total the numbers circled in the space provided.

A score between 90 and 100 indicates you should be leading successful discussions. Scores between 70 and 89 indicate significant strengths plus a few improvement needs. A score between 50 and 69 reflects some strengths, but a significant number of problem areas as well. Scores below 50 call for a serious effort to improve in several categories. Make a special effort to grow in any area where you scored 6 or less regardless of your total score.

1. I let the employee do most of the talking.   10 9 8 7 6 5 4 3 2 1

2. I make an intense effort to listen to the employee's ideas.   10 9 8 7 6 5 4 3 2 1

3. I am prepared to suggest solutions to problems and development needs but let the employee contribute first.   10 9 8 7 6 5 4 3 2 1

4. My statements about performance are descriptive, not judgemental.   10 9 8 7 6 5 4 3 2 1

5. I reinforce the positives in performance as well as seeking ways to eliminate the negatives.   10 9 8 7 6 5 4 3 2 1

6. I try to support the employee's ideas rather than force my own.   10 9 8 7 6 5 4 3 2 1

7. I invite alternatives rather than assume there is only one way to approach an issue.   10 9 8 7 6 5 4 3 2 1

8. I use open-ended, reflective and directive questions to stimulate discussion.   10 9 8 7 6 5 4 3 2 1

9. I am specific and descriptive when I express a concern about performance.   10 9 8 7 6 5 4 3 2 1

10. My employees know I want them to succeed.   10 9 8 7 6 5 4 3 2 1

TOTAL _____

Both parties agree on a performance plan for the next period and summarise these agreements.

WRAPPING IT UP

CHAPTER 19
Closing the Appraisal Discussion

When the supervisor and employee have concluded discussion of past performance, addressed any development needs and established new goals and/or standards for the future, they need to take time to review these agreements and plans. Many performance reviews fail because participants end the session with differing perceptions about what was accomplished and what was agreed. To prevent this the leader should conclude the discussion by:

1. Summarising what has been discussed and agreed. This should be done positively and enthusiastically.
2. Giving the employee a chance to react, question, and add additional ideas and suggestions.
3. Expressing appreciation for the employee's participation and reinforcing the commitment to future plans.
4. Following the discussion with a written record of the agreements and/or required action plans.

EMPLOYEE RESPONSE TO THE APPRAISAL MAY DIFFER FROM WHAT YOU EXPECT

It is a good idea, therefore, to give some thought to the range of possible responses in advance, and make plans accordingly.

How would you respond to the employee behaviour described in the following case studies?

CHAPTER 20
Case Studies

Here are some situations about ways employees responded to their appraisal. After reading each example, indicate how you would react.

Situation 1

> The employee agrees with the appraisal and wants to improve. Some genuine differences of opinion are expressed, but the employee makes positive efforts to clarify the issues rather than be defensive.

Your response _____

_____

_____

_____

_____

Situation 2

> The employee does not accept responsibility for his substandard performance and blames company politics and other employees.

Your response _____

_____

_____

_____

_____

Situation 3

> The employee disagrees with elements of your appraisal and offers specific information to refute your findings.

Your response _____

_____

_____

_____

_____

Situation 4

> The employee accepts the appraisal without saying a word
> and prepares to leave before you have discussed the next
> performance plan.

Your response _____

_____

_____

_____

_____

Compare your responses with the author's on pages 73–4.

PART 4

Following up

Three Suggestions for Following up

1. Written records

Once the performance appraisal discussion has been concluded, a manager should immediately make a written record of:

- the overall appraisal for the previous period;
- plans which both parties agreed to;
- any personal commitments requiring specific action.

A copy of this summary should be given to the employee.

2. Reflection

Following each review is a good time to review your performance in leading the discussion. Some good questions are:

- What was done well?
- What was done poorly?
- What will be done differently next time?
- What was learned about the employee?
- What was learned about self and job?

3. Follow through

A third element of follow-up is to ensure that agreements are kept and plans followed. If this is not done, the entire appraisal loses its impact and the employee assumes no one cares very much about performance. This phase of the follow-up is actually the initial phase of the next appraisal.

> To review what you have read, and to plan your next performance appraisal, study the checklist on the next two pages.

A Performance Appraisal Checklist for Managers

The following checklist is designed to guide the manager in preparing, conducting and following through employee performance appraisal discussions.

1. Personal preparation

☐ I have reviewed mutually understood expectations with respect to job duties, projects, goals, standards, and any other predetermined performance factors pertinent to this appraisal discussion.

☐ I have observed job performance measured against mutually understood expectations. In so doing, I have done my best to avoid such pitfalls as:
____ Bias/prejudice
____ The vagaries of memory
____ Over-attention to some aspects of the job at the expense of others
____ Being influenced too much by my own experience
____ Trait evaluation rather than performance measurement

☐ I have reviewed the employee's background including:
____ Skills
____ Work experience
____ Training

☐ I have identified the employee's performance strengths and areas in need of improvement and in so doing have:

———— Accumulated specific, unbiased documentation that can be used to help communicate my position

———— Limited myself to those critical points that are the most important

———— Prepared a possible development plan in case the employee needs assistance in coming up with a suitable plan

☐ I have identified areas for concentration in setting goals and standards for the next appraisal period.

☐ I have given the employee advance notice of when the discussion will be held so that he or she can prepare.

☐ I have set aside an adequate block of uninterrupted time to permit a full and complete discussion.

2. Conducting the appraisal discussion

☐ I plan to begin the discussion by creating a sincere, but open and friendly atmosphere. This includes:

———— Reviewing the purpose of the discussion

———— Making it clear that it is a joint discussion for the purpose of mutual problem-solving and goal setting

———— Striving to put the employee at ease

☐ In the body of the discussion I intend to keep the focus on job performance and related factors. This includes:

———— Discussing job requirements – employee strengths, accomplishments, improvement needs and evaluating results of performance against objectives set during previous reviews and discussions

———— Being prepared to cite observations for each point I want to discuss

_____ Encouraging the employee to appraise his or her own performance

_____ Using open, reflective and directive questions to promote thought, understanding and problem solving

☐ I will encourage the employee to outline his or her personal plans for self-development before suggesting ideas of my own. In the process, I will:

_____ Try to get the employee to set personal growth and improvement targets

_____ Strive to reach agreement on appropriate development plans which detail what the employee intends to do, a timetable, and support I am prepared to give

☐ I am prepared to discuss work assignments, projects and goals for the next appraisal period and will ask the employee to come prepared with suggestions.

3. Closing the discussion

☐ I will be prepared to make notes during the discussion for the purpose of summarising agreements and follow up. In closing, I will:

_____ Summarise what has been discussed

_____ Show enthusiasm for plans that have been made

_____ Give the employee an opportunity to make additional suggestions

_____ End on a positive, friendly, harmonious note

4. Post-appraisal follow-up

☐ As soon as the discussion is over, I will record the plans made, points requiring follow-up, the commitments I made, and provide a copy for the employee.

☐ I will also evaluate how I handled the discussion.

_____ What I did well

_____ What I could have done better

_____ What I learned about the employee and his or her job

_____ What I learned about myself and my job

Reflect for a moment on what you have been learning – then develop an action plan to apply the concepts. The guide on the next page may help.

Think over the material in this book: the self-analysis questionnaires; the case studies; and the reinforcement exercises. What did you learn about performance appraisals? What did you learn about yourself? How can you apply what you learned? Make a commitment to become better at performance appraisals. Design a personal action plan to help accomplish this goal.

The actual plan on the facing page may help clarify your goals, and outline appropriate action to achieve those goals.

A Personal Action Plan

1. My appraisal skills are strong in the following areas:

   _____

   _____

   _____

   _____

2. I need to improve the following appraisal skills:

   _____

   _____

   _____

   _____

3. My appraisal improvement goals are: (Be sure they are specific, attainable and measurable.)

   _____

   _____

   _____

   _____

4. Here are my actions steps to accomplish my goals.

   _____

   _____

   _____

   _____

   NAME

Author's Suggested Answers to Cases

Who will be best at performance appraisals?

With proper training and guidance, Janice and Frank may both become excellent at performance appraisal. At this point, however, Janice has better instincts about how an appraisal should be approached. Employees need to know what is expected of them. When employees have an opportunity to participate in establishing goals and standards they usually make good contributions. Contrary to Frank's assumption, workers tend to set goals and standards too high rather than too low.

What upset Jack

Jack may be upset because Diane seems to have an attitude that reflects 'I know best – what could you possibly contribute to this discussion of your performance?' Jack was asked to leave a meeting to come in for his appraisal discussion. This may have embarrassed him. It also suggests the discussion had not been scheduled in advance so he had no opportunity to prepare. Diana's approach seems to be 'Here's what is wrong and here's what to do about it'. Jack has no opportunity for questions or input. How would you react under similar circumstances?

Situation 1

Express gratitude for the employee's active participation. This employee has voiced the expected response if you follow the process described in this book. Most employees want information about their strengths and weaknesses, and how to invest their time more profitably for improvement. Don't forget the importance of sincere praise when it is earned.

Situation 2

Listen with an open mind. Without interrupting or arguing, try to find out why the person is placing the blame elsewhere. Then move the discussion towards corrective action that can be achieved with the employee's cooperation. Compliment the employee any time a move is made towards accepting responsibility. Follow up closely and schedule another review soon to measure changes in the employee's point of view.

Situation 3

Listen carefully to the employee. Then indicate your willingness to re-examine your data. If it turns out that the employee's information is more valid than yours, modify your position accordingly. If you believe the employee's data is invalid, or irrelevant, stand your ground and explain your position.

Situation 4

Some individuals are intimidated by the appraisal process and a special effort is required to open things up. Others may feel a quick agreement will save them from a discussion of their faults. When employees are reluctant to talk, encourage them by asking questions. As them to suggest activities which would help them. Ask them to summarise their performance. Ask for their conclusions at the end of the session. Ensure they provide input on their new performance plan.

Also Available from Kogan Page